[Type text]

DO OUR
LITTLE SINS
REALLY
COUNT?

Helen Glowacki

Novels by Helen Glowacki
When God Broke Grandma's Heart
When God Took Grandma Home
When Grandma Chased the Spirits
The Granddaughter and the Monkey Swing
Grandma's Little Book of Poetry: The Story of God's Plan
of Salvation
Abiding Faith, Hidden Treasure
And Then They Asked God
Caleb's Testimony

Why God Why Series by Helen Glowacki
To What Purpose?
Why God Why?
Why Trust Scripture?
What Should I Know About Life after Death And
The Coming Tribulation?
What Does God Want Me To Do RIGHT NOW?
Do Our Little Sins *Really* Count?

Other non-fiction Books by Helen Glowacki
Politically Incorrect: The Get Some Gumption
Handbook When Enough is Enough
Overcoming Depression: How to be Happy
What No One Is Telling You about Addictions

****

Authors Website: www.Helenglowacki.com
Face book: http://www.facebook.com/pages/The-
Grandmother-Series/155300907853909?ref=ts

DO OUR
LITTLE SINS
REALLY
COUNT?

Helen Glowacki

<u>MISSION STATEMENT</u>

To Serve

God

With All Our Strength

And

All Our Heart

Helen Glowacki

NOTE TO THE READER

The novels by Helen Glowacki are works of fiction. While some events in these novels reflect the expertise and support of those in particular vocations, references to real people, events, organizations, or locales are intended only to provide a sense of authenticity, and are used fictitiously. Characters, incidents and dialogue are drawn from the author's imagination and are not to be construed as real. Any resemblance to actual persons, living or dead is entirely coincidental.

The non-fiction books by Helen Glowacki represent the opinion, research, religious beliefs and scriptural interpretations of the author and not meant to be used in lieu of the advice of ministerial, theological, medical or psychological experts.

The King James Version (KJV) of the Bible, which is public domain in the United States, is used throughout all the books written by this author. For further study, the author recommends the New King James Version (NKJV) of the Bible as easier reading and less usage of the old world language while remaining true to the original text.

ACKNOWLEDGEMENTS

Special thanks to my husband Wally who provides so much support to my work and makes my computer behave. Thanks to my children and grandchildren for the constancy of their love and encouragement, and to Reverend Herold Ambroise for his fervent prayers on my behalf. Special thanks to Richard Levinson for providing the first opportunity through which I could develop my writing skills, to my brothers and sisters and ministers in faith who give so freely of their love and prayers, and to my Face book friends who also pray for me and support this ministry. My thanks to Katharina Leipp, Muhlaker, Germany for her friendship, her support of my work and for translating the novel *Caleb's Testimony* and my many articles into the German language. Thanks also to Darren Robinson, for his meticulous assembly of the cover and to Daniel Patrick Landolfi for maintaining the website. But most of all, my heartfelt, humble thanks to our Heavenly Father for His inspiration, guiding hand, protection, and never-ending love. May this work bring joy to His heart and help find that last soul!

"One thing have I

desired of the Lord,

that I will seek after;

that I may dwell

in the house of the Lord

all the days of my life,

to behold the beauty of the Lord,

and to enquire in his temple."

Psalm 27: 4

MESSAGE FROM THE AUTHOR

Most of us try to live according to the rules of society and by the tenets of our personal beliefs. But sometimes our actions do not fit into a "definitely right or definitely wrong" category. While it is not difficult to avoid actions which are *blatantly* wrong, it is difficult to avoid the little things which never seem "wrong enough". There are also times when we are fully aware that what we have said or done is not pleasing to God, but rather than acknowledge our shortcomings we find an excuse for our behavior. Sometimes we compare what we do to what someone else has done and decide that our actions are not any worse. Or perhaps we determine that it will be of little consequence if we add "just a little more" to our list of borderline behaviors. Sadly, as we rationalize these away, we become confused and no longer view *all* sin as a detriment to our future with God. We slip into a general acceptance of our "little" faults and no longer view them as potentially dangerous to our soul salvation. We excuse our behavior so quickly that we hardly notice that we have strayed from the path God wants us to take. While these begin with deeds which are not earth shattering, as we slide effortlessly into the smaller sins, we open ourselves up to accepting the larger ones. These choices originate from the selfish Adam-like nature with which we are born. That nature is filled with a pride which easily finds justification for every action. It is found in every person old or young, rich or poor.

The true children of God however, are those who voluntarily battle *every day* to defeat that nature. Thus, the difference between someone who is striving to be and remain a child of God is that one actively seeks to know and please God and the other shrugs off any momentary pang of guilt by justifying what they do. Without knowing what scripture tells us and therefore not knowing what God asks of His children, it is difficult to recognize everything we do which can harm our ability to become the bride of Christ.. Thus many live their lives steeped in a complacency they do not realize exists. God, in His loving kindness, works to open our understanding of His plan of salvation and the pre-requisites He has laid out for His children. He wants us to be aware of those things He will look for in the bride. While God forgives our errors, He looks for our heart's attitude and how much we desire, and therefore *strive* to learn of Him and His precepts. He looks at the depth of our effort to mold ourselves into the self-sacrificing nature of Christ by shedding the self-centered Adam-like nature with which we are born. Unless we know what God says, we cannot learn, nor do what He asks. His plan is open to all of mankind and He has given man the free will to come to Him ....or not. He is aware of the very sly and seductive nature of evil which blinds us to the truth unless we learn of its power and why it seeks to entrap us. Once we learn these truths, what seemed unimportant suddenly looms as that which we recognize as the sins we have not acknowledged. Confusion and distraction are evil's allies, thus we require God's help to know why we sin and how sin can prevent us from participating in the future God plans for us. Many ask if our good intentions are more important than the sins we commit and if so, why do we need to overcome every little thing we do wrong? But scripture tells us that God expects us to "work" to overcome right up to the moment Christ returns and that if we do, He will forgive all our sin so the Bride of Christ can be perfect. Scripture also tells us what the difference is between the "lambs" who will enter heaven and the "Bride" or "Firstlings" who will be a part of the First Resurrection. It tells us that, although we all commit sin and will continue to do so until Satan is bound we are nevertheless required to take certain steps to assure that we *can* be forgiven. All that we need to know is contained in scripture, and as the marvel of God's plan for our future is revealed, we recognize a love which our world is not capable of, and we long to be a part of that love. This book will discuss the many facets of sin, how sin relates to God's plan for mankind, and what we must strive for to please God. It will explain why Holy Communion can be taken either worthily or unworthily, why our sins of omission also count, why inherited sin is important to us and to our children, and why the seven deadly sins are so insidious. I hope you like this sixth book in my Why God Why mini-series. I hope that it answers some of your questions about sin, about the forgiveness of sin, and how we grow into what God wants in His children. If you do like this book, I ask that you share what you have learned with others. And I wish for you God's richest blessings.

Helen Glowacki

TABLE OF CONTENTS

> *"And thou shalt teach them ordinances and laws, and shall shew them the way wherein they must walk, and the work they must do". Exodus 18:20*

Chapter One

THE TEN COMMANDMENTS

Most of us believe that it's the large sins which God will count and that it's simply human nature to commit the smaller sins. Yet scripture tells us that God seeks those who will be a *perfect* bride for His Son. Just as our spouse, children, and friends may be well aware of our faults, so too would the bridegroom with whom we hope to share our future. Thus perhaps our little sins *are* important and that whatever we do, say and think should be examined in the light of how the Lord Jesus would look upon them. While we are assured that we will be forgiven our sins when the Lord returns for His Bride, we may not be forgiven the sins for which we have no remorse.

Scripture describes those who Christ will take at the First Resurrection as "overcomers". This infers that we have done the work to uncover our sins and that we will desire and strive to "go and sin no more". If so, Matthew 25:21 promises: *".....thou hast been faithful over a few things, I will make thee ruler over many..."*

When Adam and Eve were placed into the Garden of Eden they were given only one commandment to follow. This was: *"Of every tree of the garden thou mayest freely eat: but of the tree of the knowledge of good and evil, thou shalt not eat of it: for in the day that thou eatest thereof thou shalt surely die.* (Genesis 2:16-17) Nevertheless, even with only this one rule in place, Adam and Eve were tempted by Satan, who took the form of a serpent, and they ate of that tree. This meant that they would no longer have fellowship with God and would have to face death. God had originally given man free will so that they could *choose* to love Him and to follow His precepts *voluntarily*. But once Adam and Eve sinned and thereby experienced spiritual death by losing their access to God, they were doomed to experience the effects of evil and to be separated from God for all eternity. But God, knowing what Satan would do, provided a way for man to return to Him...through the sacrifice of Christ. Nevertheless, because Adam chose to sample evil, man was to experience evil throughout his lifetime. He would eventually use his free will to choose between good (God) and evil (Satan). To help man live in harmony with one another and to live as God deigned, God gave Moses the Ten Commandments which he was to teach his followers. The Ten Commandments were one of three sets of laws to which man was subjected. One was the law of nature which were those things which function in our world without the influence of man but which man can transgress by unnatural activities. Another was the moral laws of the Ten Commandments which God gave to Moses to teach man what activities were and were not acceptable to God. (Exodus 20:1-17) And another was the law designed by a temporal authority such as a king or a government under which a society formed.

The Ten Commandments represented a covenant between God and man whereby God promised that if man followed these rules they would find favor with Him. God also provided these rules so man could live in harmony with his neighbor. There was no grace available to mankind during this era therefore there was no forgiveness of sin. Grace began after Christ sacrificed His life for mankind. The commandments are as follows:

1. *"Thou shalt have no other Gods before me".*
2. *"Thou shalt not make unto thee any graven image........"*
3. *"Thou shalt not bow down thyself to them, nor serve them, for I the Lord am a jealous God, visiting the iniquity of the fathers upon the children unto the third and fourth generation of them that hate me......"*
4. *"Thou shalt not take the name of the Lord thy God in vain......"*
5. *"Remember the Sabbath day, to keep it holy......do not do any work......"*
6. *"Honour thy father and thy mother....."*
7. *"Thou shalt not kill."*
8. *"Thou shalt not steal."*
9. *"Thou shalt not bear false witness...."*
10. *"Thou shalt not covet thy neighbors house....wife....manservant.....maidservant .....ox....ass....nor anything that is thy neighbors."*

When these laws were given to Moses, Satan was still actively seeking to destroy man's relationship with God. Therefore he wanted man to break these rules so that he would be separated from God. Satan's power over mankind is clearly explained in scripture: Satan has the power to move men to do his bidding (1 Chronicles 21:1), walk back and forth on the earth (Job 1:7), cause illness (Job 2:7), take God's word from men's hearts (Mark 4:15), enter man (Luke 22:3), blind the minds of them which believe not (John 13:27), transform himself (2 Corinthians 4:4), send messengers to hurt man (2 Corinthians 11:14), hinder people (2 Corinthians 12:7), produce signs and has powers (1 Thessalonians 2:18), and uses his power to convince man to accept his perversions. (2 Thessalonians 2:9).

Knowing what man faced, God made provision for those who loved Him and desired to do His will, yet had died in sin. He provided them with the opportunity to have their sins forgiven in eternity after Christ made His sacrifice for them. Peter 4:6 tells us: *". . . for this cause was the gospel preached also, **to them that are dead**, that they might be judged according to men in the flesh, but live according to God in the spirit."* This verse and many others indicate that when Christ died, he brought the testimony of his sacrifice and the grace offered through His death to those in all realms of hell before ascending to heaven. Ephesians 4:8-10 reveals: *"Wherefore he saith, When he ascended up on high, he led captivity captive, and gave gifts unto men. (Now that he ascended, what is it but that **he also descended first into the lower parts of the earth?** He that descended is the same also that ascended up far above all heavens, that he might fill all things.)"*

1 Peter 3:18-20 tells us: *For Christ also hath once suffered for sins, the just for the unjust, that he might bring us to God, being put to death in the*

flesh, but quickened by the Spirit: By which also He went and **preached unto the spirits in prison***; Which sometime were disobedient, when once the longsuffering of God waited* **in the days of Noah** *. . .*" And John 5:25 reveals: , *"Verily, verily, I say unto you, The hour is coming, and now is, when* **the dead shall hear** *the voice of the Son of God: and they that shall hear shall live."*

What we learn from these verses is that when Christ made the sacrifice to redeem man by paying the ransom for his sins, grace became available to those who were alive *and* those who had died in sin prior to the time of His sacrifice. Scripture uses the words *"they that shall hear"* which indicates that these were souls who *desired* forgiveness after hearing the testimony Christ brought to them. Sadly, many of the souls in eternity did not accept Christ's offer just as they do not accept His offer of grace here on earth at this present time.

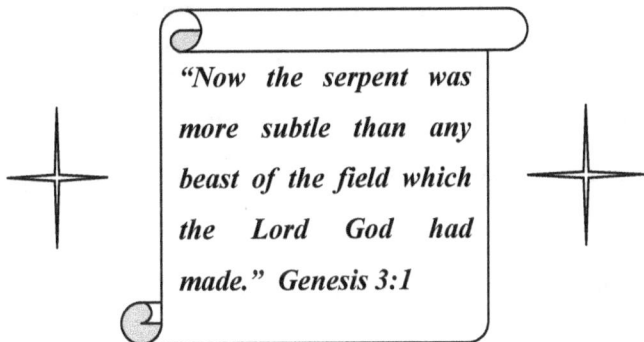

> *"Now the serpent was more subtle than any beast of the field which the Lord God had made." Genesis 3:1*

Chapter Two

THE SEVEN DEADLY SINS

The previous chapter addressed the fall of Adam and Eve, and spoke of the time when Moses brought mankind the Ten Commandments. We should also note that in Noah's time, God brought a great flood to the earth to destroy mankind because of the magnitude of their sin. Christ had not yet appeared, and therefore sin could not be bridged. God made the decision to save only the few in Noah's family who were faithful to Him, and destroyed all others to slow the rampant growth of sin which was occurring at that time. He also did this to preserve the line of Noah, who were the descendants through which Christ would come. But when God saw the multitudes of sinners who entered Hades, it grieved Him and He made a covenant not to destroy mankind again until the end times. Thus, after the flood, sin again grew unfettered until Christ came to pay the price for man's redemption. Christ came to earth to usher in the era of love and to sacrifice His life for the living and for those who had died in the era of the law. This meant that those who lived under the Law of Moses or in the time of Noah would have the opportunity to be saved. It included all the souls who lived during the entire 5,000 years before Christ appeared and gave His life for mankind. His sacrifice was for everyone who had ever been conceived, lived or died who would accept His offer of salvation. Therefore when Christ died on the cross, He went to the *dead* for three days and then to the Apostles still here on earth *before* ascending to God. His mission was to tell the dead of His sacrifice and offer them salvation. He also spent time to instruct, convince and comfort His Apostles before He ascended to God so that the Apostles of Christ would continue His work of salvation on earth. However, just as some accepted God's offer and others did not here on earth, some in hell accepted and others did not...and this still holds true today. Therefore we live in a time when sin is again rampant and man does not acknowledge his sins and neither does he have remorse for them. Many have no knowledge of God's plan of salvation, and few seek to learn of God. As a result, Satan can work his subtle magic of complacency to keep man from God in the hope that he can forestall the time when he will be bound. Sadly, many of us never think in terms of an evil entity which is capable of invading man, nor of us being so weak as to succumb to such beings. We may not even realize when we are battling a satanic spirit. We respond to what people say and do with little understanding that we should respond instead to what these spiritual entitles may *cause* them to say or do. Our misunderstanding allows us to become the pawns or playthings of these spirits as we struggle against situations which we don't accept as evil at work. Scripture warns us in Hosea 4:6: *"My people are destroyed for lack of knowledge; because thou hast rejected knowledge, I will also reject thee, that thou shall be no priest to me: seeing thou hast forgotten the law of thy God, I will also forget thy children."* This verse and many others throughout scripture clearly explain that without an understanding of what scripture tells us, we cannot know how to do battle with evil. However, if we do learn God's words, we find that God explains evil and tells us how to fight against it. He tells us to love all souls; even those being influenced by evil. God teaches through scripture that mankind can be owned and directed by satanic influence and once free of that influence might be open to changing their lives. For this reason, we grieve God when we waste our time and energy fighting the wrong battles against a captive soul and therefore lose the real battle against the entity which directs them. First and foremost we must understand why Satan does what he does and what power he employs to work his evil. In John 8:44 we are told, *"...... for he is a liar and the father of it."* And in John 8:44, *"........He was a murderer from the beginning, and abode not in the truth, because there is no truth in him......"* This clearly indicates that we must be on guard against the lies evil tells which distract us from the real issue we must face. Satan loves the anonymity of working in secret to keep us from God. He wants us to hate and judge and condemn... not Satan, but the souls he has invaded. He is so subtle that many cannot believe that he exists. Genesis 3:1 tells us, *"..... the serpent was more subtil than any beast......"* These prior three verses alone teach that Satan is a liar, a murderer, (of men's souls) and is subtle in his attacks. Matthew 4:1 adds that Satan also tempts us. He is actually called "the tempter". *"Then was Jesus led...... to be tempted of the devil."* And in Matthew 4: 3 *"and when the tempter came to Him, he said....."* Thus we know that Satan has power, is unscrupulous in what he does and wants to separate us from God. We must therefore watch for those sins which we may not easily recognize. Some of these sins are among what are termed the seven deadly sins. These are pride, envy, sloth, anger, greed, lust and gluttony. Envy, greed, and lust easily fit into our understanding of the tenth commandment which says: *"Thou shalt not covet thy neighbors house.... wife.... manservant..... maidservant..... ox.... .ass.... nor anything that is thy neighbors."*. Each of these sins can correlate to one of the Ten Commandments but are so subtle that we seldom recognize them as sins. To do so we must look for the virtues with which we can counteract these sins. These are: humility as opposed to pride, favor as opposed to envy, zeal as opposed to sloth, love as opposed to anger, generosity as opposed to greed, and self-control as opposed to lust. If we examine even one of these words...pride.... we can learn from scripture how important these sins are.

There are at least 49 verses in scripture which contain the word pride. Each of these condemns pride as an attitude which is displeasing to God, and defiling to man. Webster's Dictionary defines the word pride as "inordinate self-esteem, conceit, delight or elation with a position, possession or relationship, disdainful, and haughty". Roget's Thesaurus lists the words "egotism", "arrogant" and "regarding oneself with undue favor" as synonyms. There are many reasons why we develop pride. Often it is because of an asset we project to others such as beauty, intelligence, wealth, talent, power, position or eloquent speech. Ironically, these are gifts which God gave us, not those we developed ourselves or through hard work and perseverance. Being proud of an accomplishment toward which we labored and for which we thank God is very different than exhibiting pride to exalt ourselves above others.

As we read the verses in scripture which address pride, we learn that in most of them God warns that those with pride will be brought down. Isaiah 25:11 tells us *"And he shall spread forth his hands in the midst of them, as he that swimmeth spreadeth forth his hands to swim; and he shall bring down their pride together with the spoils of their hands."* Daniel 5:20 warns, *"But when his heart was lifted up, and his mind hardened in pride, he was deposed from his kingly throne, and they took his glory from him."* Obadiah 2-4 tells us, *"Behold, I have made thee small.....thou art greatly despised....The pride of thy heart hath deceived thee....though thou exalt thyself as the eagle....I bring thee down saith the Lord."* Proverbs tells us that pride is a spirit which is evil and must be exorcized from our heart. Specifically, Proverbs 16:18 tells us, *"Pride goweth before destruction, and a haughty spirit before a fall.*" Proverbs 8:13 says, "*The fear of the Lord is to hate evil: pride, and arrogancy, and the evil way, and the forward mouth do I hate.*" Proverbs 11:2 tells us, "*When pride cometh, then cometh shame....*" Proverbs 29:23 warns, "*A man's pride shall bring him low....*" Zephaniah also makes reference to pride as emanating evil when it says that pride is from a "god of the earth". Zephaniah 2:10-11 tells us, "*This shall they have for their pride, because they have reproached and magnified themselves against the people of the Lord of hosts. The Lord will be terrible unto them; for he will famish the gods of the earth.....*" Defining pride as evil is also addressed in Mark 7:20-23 where we are told, "*....That which cometh out of the man, that defileth the man. For from within, out of the heart of men, proceed evil thoughts...an evil eye....pride....All these evil things come from within and defile the man.*" All of the warnings about pride can be summed up in two verses, one from 1

John and another from 1 Timothy. The verse from 1 John 2:16 tells us: *"For all that is in the world, the lust of the flesh, and the lust of the eyes, and the pride of life, is not of the Father, but is of the world. And the world passeth away, and the lust thereof: but he that doeth the will of God abideth forever."* And the verse from 1 Timothy 3:6 warns, *"....lest being lifted up with pride he fall into the condemnation of the devil."* What these verses reveal is that there is far more to sin than first meets the eye. The true definition of love is to want to do that which pleases the one we love. Therefore we must carefully view our activities through the fruits of the Holy Spirit. We must be sure that everything we do engages love, joy, peace, longsuffering, gentleness, goodness, faith, meekness, and temperance which are the fruits of the Holy Spirit. (Galatians 5:22, 23). We are told *"If we live in the Spirit, let us also walk in the Spirit. Let us not be desirous of vain glory, provoking one another, envying one another."* (Galatians 6:25, 26)

"All scripture is given by inspiration of God, and is profitable for doctrine, for reproof, for correction, for instruction in righteousness."
11 Timothy 3:16

Chapter Three

SINS OF COMMISSION

Faith has the power to heal and prayer often produces a miracle. Further, scripture tells us in Proverbs 3:8 that to know and acknowledge God is *"...health to thy navel, and marrow to thy bones."* But interestingly, our self esteem is also increased when we have a strong faith in God and a close relationship with Him. Our self esteem correlates with our trust that God loves us, looks after us, and has forgiven the sins we have committed. A strong and godly self esteem helps us stand up for our faith and demonstrates our faith in God's promises. These strengths can only exist when we understand what God asks of us, understand what role Satan plays in our lives, and we truly believe in the power of forgiveness through what Christ did for us. A lack of self esteem however, is often found in those who do not have this knowledge and therefore do not know why they sin, or why God forgives them, or even what is required to take Holy Communion worthily. They fall prey to the insecurities which spawn anger, hate and envy, and a need for revenge. They dredge up the past so often that they remember every real or imagined slight and begin to think that they must seek restitution. They are fearful of expressing their innermost thoughts and do not know the difference between righteous and unrighteous anger. Some mistakenly believe that to be a child of God, one must never be angry or cause others to become angry and must be tolerant and forgiving in *all* things thus often *supports* sinful activities. However, this is not what scripture tells us. This leads to a confusion which increases a lack of self esteem. Confusion is the prime reason why some have little confidence in what God will do for them. Without the ability to trust God's plan and our role in that plan, we cannot know the extent of God's love or what Christ endured on our behalf. When we are unsure of ourselves and unsure that our sins are forgiven or cannot accept that our sins have been forgiven or overcome, we fall prey to our worries and insecurities and soon accept the lies which Satan tells us to break our faith. Sins of commission are not only those actions which we easily see as wrong, but also those actions which cause us to step back when we should step up. When we consciously *choose* not to learn God's words, it is a sin of commission. Further, scripture tells us that when we interact with someone who is engaged in an activity which is displeasing to God we should express anger, rebuke them, and provide them with sound speech and doctrine. Titus 1:10

tells us, *"For there are many unruly and vain talkers and deceivers...."* And in Titus 1:16 *"They profess that they know God; but in works they deny him, being abominable, and disobedient, and unto every good work reprobate."* Titus 2:7-8 tells us: *"In all things shewing thyself a pattern of good works: in doctrine showing uncorruptness, gravity, sincerity. Sound speech that cannot be condemned; that he that is of the contrary part may be ashamed, having no evil thing to say of you.* And Titus 2:15 tells us, *"These things speak, and exhort, and rebuke with all authority...."* However, if we do not know God's words or what is meant by them, we are unable to speak with authority and are bereft of the information needed to successfully stand as a child of God. Therefore we retreat or worse, espouse those sins in the name of tolerance and love. These actions feed the spirit of evil and grieve the Holy Spirit and result in an increase in our lack of self esteem. We understand that we *should* know God's words, *should* stand up for our faith and have no viable excuse for not doing so. It is the Adam-like nature which seeks to avoid the embarrassment of admitting how remiss we have been and to hide the failure to address those who attack God or godly principles. We then view ourselves as timid or cowardly or uninformed or compensate by telling ourselves that we have acted with tolerance. The psychological ramifications are great when we continue to brush aside our duty, especially our duty to God who clearly warns in Hosea 4:6: *"My people are destroyed for lack of knowledge......"* This verse applies to every issue a child of God faces and is the core reason we fail God and fail to help others. It is why we often suffer from an insecurity which we cover up with an arrogant attitude. These actions, along with the more blatant actions which we know are displeasing to God, are just as deadly. These too are sins of commission and by committing these...without asking for forgiveness, we may not be found worthy. We need then to look for these sins and to ask God to help us correct them. Without self esteem, without a sense of who we are and what we stand for, we will never be effective in our faith. A lack of self-esteem, which grows out of a lack of understanding, can harm every aspect of our lives. It can grow into resentment and depression and adversely affect our relationship with spouse and children, friends and business associates. Scripture even tells us that to know and acknowledge God is *"...health to thy navel, and marrow to thy bones."* (Proverbs 3:8) And, as previously mentioned Hosea 4:6 warns us: *"My people are destroyed for lack of knowledge......"* Proverbs 3:3-6 tells us, *"Let not mercy and truth forsake thee; bind them about thy neck; write them upon the table of thine heart. So shalt thou find favor and good understanding in the sight of God and man. Trust in the Lord with all thine heart; and lean not to your own understanding. In all thy ways, acknowledge him and he shall direct thy paths."* When scripture uses the word truth it refers to the word of God.

Scripture teaches that unless everything we do, think and say is based on the word of God, we will be unable to discern between perverted doctrine and sound wisdom. Without knowing the word of God we will stumble in our walk of faith. Proverbs 3:23 tells us, *"Then shall thou walk in thy way safely, and thy foot shall not stumble. When thou liest down, thou shalt not be afraid: yea, thou shall lie down, and thy sleep shall be sweet.* Proverbs 3:26 promises, *"For the Lord shall be thy confidence, and shall keep thy foot from being taken."* These words assure us that if we learn God's words, do our best to apply them, and speak them, we will never have to be afraid and will never lack confidence. Philippians 4:7 assures us, *"And the peace of God, which passeth all understanding, shall keep your hearts and minds through Jesus Christ."* Philippians 4:19 says, *"......God shall supply all your need......"* And 1 Peter 5:7 tells us, *"Casting all your care upon him; for he careth for you."* We must cast off all confusion, not overlook these hidden sins, nor be tolerant of sin unless there is remorse and the effort to change. We must stand up for godly principles and become a beacon of stedfastness without withholding forgiveness. We must be longsuffering and patient even when we feel or express anger, and we must not judge nor seek revenge. We can pray and seek direction from scripture which will also increase our self-esteem. God promises His never ending help when we learn His words and apply them. No one can ask for better promises and no one can provide a better gift to their children than by teaching them these truths. Thus, to gain self-esteem, to conquer self doubt and avoid the psychological ramifications of fear and anxiety which today's society imposes on us, we need to immerse ourselves in the word of God. Then we will stand in confidence to fight for our faith using God's own words. He will reward us with the self-esteem we need to bring forth our strength and courage….and prove our loyalty.

> *"Then opened he their understanding that they might understand the scriptures."*
> **Luke 24:45**

Chapter Four

SINS OF OMISSION

There are many who feel assured that they have a relationship with God because they believe in God, believe that Christ died for them, and are "good people". While these are commendable and God appreciates these virtues, they do not offer God the kind of relationship he longs for. Revelation 3:15–16 warns: *"I know thy works, that thou art neither cold nor hot: I would thou wert cold or hot. So then because thou art lukewarm, and neither cold nor hot, I will spue thee out of my mouth."* To fully understand these words, we need to consider the relationship between a young married couple who are very much in love. We can learn how they interact with one another by their actions. When they fell in love, they cared so much for one another that they devised many ways to demonstrate their love. They may have placed a note into the briefcase of their spouse as a surprise to be discovered sometime during their hectic day. They might purchase a special treat for them, or telephone just to say hello or provide an endearing word. They might touch or hug when passing their spouse in a hallway or as they move from room to room. They might complete a chore for them that they had not yet found the time to complete. They would communicate intimately, share their concerns and ask what their spouses concerns are. They would talk about the good and bad parts of each day, ask advice about how to handle a particular problem and often mention how much they love them. They would discuss the purchases they wished to make and the state of their joint finances. They would act like one entity, entwined in heart and mind and spirit. They would be like-minded, appreciate one another and express that appreciation. This is what would keep them close. Every expression of love and endearment would make their hearts soar and their relationship deepen.

Their children would learn from hearing them speak to one another, from how they respond to people who hurt them, and how they show appreciation for those who support them. Their children would learn from the prayers they say aloud with one another, and their hearts would be touched by the prayers they hear from the one they love. They would be a happy family because they are openly expressive with one another. They would not be lukewarm with one another. They would articulate their love for one another and share their triumphs and burdens with one another. Therefore we must ask ourselves if we would be happy in this kind of a relationship or if we would rather have a relationship where we are treated with indifference. Would we rather love someone who is uncommunicative, acts neither hot nor cold, neither caring nor uncaring. Would we feel loved, important to that person, feel that they cared? Would our love for them become cool and lukewarm if we were treated this way?

Which type of relationship do we have with God? Do we converse with God as we do with those we love and do we do this many times each day? Do we speak to God of our difficulties and our triumphs as we would with our loved one? Do we trust God and ask His advice as we would with the one with whom we share our temporal life? Do we seek to do little things every day to show God how much we love Him as we do with the person we fell in love with? Do we make an effort to learn what pleases God as we did the one with whom we fell in love? If we do not do the things which all good relationships require we haven't yet developed the relationship with God which allows Him full entry into our hearts and minds, into our spirit and our future. And if we haven't yet developed that relationship, we really don't know Him. If we have not developed that degree of intimacy with God, we will be classified as lukewarm toward God, and He will rightly say that He knows us not. This is an omission on our part.

We can bring very little to God, but what we can bring is an open heart. We can also teach our children about God and we can love those God loves and reach out to help them. God wants to develop a bride for His Son, and inhabitants for His new heaven and new earth who will truly desire to give and show love. How then can He accept those who are not willing to work for the kind of a relationship with Him that exists between a man and a woman who are deeply in love? How can we love someone with whom we share no time or effort?

This too is a sin of omission which we all commit at one time or another. Only we can answer this question about the relationship we have fostered with God and what we *could* be doing to love those who God loves to demonstrate our loyalty and appreciation for what He has given us. Each of us must learn what love really is. Each of us must not pass up the opportunities God provides where we can offer our love to others, where we can teach and encourage, where we can uplift and be an example.

Love is expressed when we whisper the words "Thank You" to our Heavenly Father many times each day. It is expressed when we find ourselves angry yet bite our tongue and then tell our Heavenly Father that we are trying to live as He asks us to live and request His help. Love is the trust with which we describe our worries to Him and ask Him to guide us, trusting that He will. Love is the intimacy through which we ask Him to bless us and teach us and protect us every day. Love is having the courage to stand firm and fight to retain the values and treasures He has given us. Love is being willing to reach out to others.

As parents we learn through scripture that we are to teach our children about God and do so from a very young age. We are also taught to help others and to be a role model who can draw others to God. Often however, our lifestyles are so busy that we simply do not make the time to do these things which scripture urges us to do. Thus in these areas we also practice the sin of omission.

While these may seem innocent enough, they may make the difference between being a lamb which will be brought into the kingdom of heaven or being the bride of Christ who will become a family member. These activities or lack thereof may be why there will be, according to scripture, such a relatively small number of souls who will be a part of the First Resurrection. But if we long to be included, we must seek to recognize and then overcome even the sins of omission. We must offer our repentance, our desire to do better in the future, give gladly both our tithing and our effort, our willingness to learn and must teach God's words, and be a help to others. This will result in a true relationship of love and trust and when we seek to recognize where we may be committing a sin of omission we will move God's heart. We will no longer sadden Him by refusing to help someone in need after He has given us so much, nor sadden Him by withholding our forgiveness when He has forgiven us so much.

Our goal must be to overcome those things which we should not do and do those things which He asks of us so we can touch God's heart as He has touched ours.

> *"Till I come, give attendance to reading, to exhortation, to doctrine. Neglect not the gift that is in thee by prophecy, with the laying on of the hands of the presbytery."*
>
> *1 Timothy 4:13*

Chapter Five

SIN BY PROXY

Few people realize that the sins of our forefathers can greatly impact our lives. It is difficult to understand why a loving God would allow this to occur. But as we study scripture we learn why God must dispel all sin, all inclination toward sin, all selfishness, envy, jealousy, hate, pride and anger from those who He will choose to enter His new kingdom. We can learn from scripture that we currently live under very specific rules of physics in a world filled with opposites and that the new world God will create for those who love Him will not be a world of opposites. From the tides to the winds, from the seasons to the harvests, from the light to the darkness we can recognize the system of opposites which govern our current world. But in God's new kingdom there will be no opposites. There will be light but no darkness, there will be love, but no hate, there will be rejoicing but no tears, there will be kindness but no anger, and there will be a harvest but no seasons as trees will bring forth a harvest every month.

God plans to abolish all sin, all hate, all darkness, and all things evil when He binds Satan (and those who do his bidding) into the lake of Fire and Brimstone for all eternity. God offers every soul who was ever conceived, born or died the opportunity to live with Him forever in His new kingdom. However, because evil will be bound, God has set forth certain rules by which a soul can enter that new kingdom. Therefore the choice to follow God or follow Satan is ours to make.

God has painstakingly taught us that sin can be instilled into one's heart by Satan and that the continued and celebrated practice of sin is the cause of the proclivity to sin in one's offspring. We learn these truths in scripture, through the sin of Adam and Eve and how this impacted all of mankind. We also learn this most notably as we follow the story of Joshua as he moves through Israel under the direct orders of God and is instructed to kill everyone who resides in certain cities while sparing other cities. We learn this as we read passages in scripture which tell us about the sins of the forefathers being visited upon the third and fourth generations of offspring. We also learn this as we read about the flood and ask ourselves why the death of certain individuals would help stop the rampant spread of sin. These passages are a part of the mystery of scripture and therefore not everyone has understood them. But when we read them with the understanding that God's desire was to keep the line from which Christ would descend a pure one, we can begin to unravel the nuances of what these verses tell us. We can also begin to understand why God so adamantly tells us to overcome sin and to guard our life of faith and… to teach these truths to our children at an early age.

Most of us feel incredible awe for the wondrous love God has for us through which He sent His Son so we could be ransomed from sin. These are the greatest gifts we could ever ask for; they are priceless….they are treasures. God has provided us with yet another gift to assist those who seek Him with an open heart. It allows us to fully understand what all His gifts mean to us by teaching us how we can reach the goal of our faith. It is the gift of scripture. Sadly, many people, believers and unbelievers alike, feel that scripture is difficult to understand. Others find scripture fascinating and timely, and appear to fully understand what they read. While many question this phenomenon, scripture clearly tells us that the Bible is a mystery whose words are not unveiled to everyone. Yet, scripture shows us the beauty and goodness which lives in the heart of God and demonstrates His emotion, His love, His goals, His plan, His desire, His righteousness, and His power. Scripture teaches us about His enemy, why that enemy seeks the destruction of our faith, and how we can protect our faith. It teaches us how to love and how we are to treat one another. But it also teaches us about sin and its everlasting danger and does so to help us become worthy to spend eternity with our Heavenly Father and with His Son. Scripture is an excellent teaching tool, and when we seek to understand what God wants to tell us, and do so with an open heart, all is revealed to us as our understanding grows and the Holy Spirit can work within us and our soul is ready to learn. One of the most fascinating components of scripture is that its wisdom is easily read and understood by many, yet hidden from others, and amazingly that more is revealed as we grow in faith. The Holy Spirit opens the secrets of scripture to those who seek them with a pure, honest and humble heart. The Holy Spirit provides this wisdom at just the right time and to those who have been "made ready" to understand its deepest elements. This is called the "mystery" of the Bible and is another component which demonstrates how much God loves us, protects us, and guides our steps toward a perfect understanding.

King David loved God so deeply that despite his many faults and failings he could always touch God's heart. He trusted God and said in Psalms 18:28, *"For thou wilt light our candle: The Lord my God will enlighten my darkness."* This was a plea from David to God for a greater understanding. His use of the word "will" indicates the trust he had that God *would* provide him with that enlightenment. Matthew 13:11 teaches us that understanding the things of God is a mystery not understood by everyone. *"Because it is given unto you to know the mysteries of the kingdom of heaven, but to them it is not given."* Further along in that chapter we learn that not all who see or hear *will* accept and follow. We also learn that God can open our understanding if we ask with a pure heart for Him to do this. Luke 24:31 tells us, *"And their eyes were opened, and they knew him....."* Sadly, some arrogantly believe that they already know all there is to know, or need only to believe, and this attitude can shortchange one's spiritual growth...and be deadly. As the Holy Spirit fills us, we are liberated from the spirits of this world which want us bound, kept from the fullness of God's truths and lazy in what we offer God. Satan uses mankind to perpetrate his evil and separate us from God. He also uses mankind to pervert the Gospel of Christ as written in scripture just enough to cause some to lose their way and to create disputes. Satan can blind the eyes of men from correctly interpreting scripture. This is why we are urged to ask God for help and ask that the Holy Spirit guide us when we read scripture.

1 Corinthians 2: 10, tells us, *"But God hath revealed them to us by his Spirit; for the Spirit searcheth all things, yea, the deep things of God."* Ephesians 3:4,5 tells us, *"Whereby, when ye read, ye may understand my knowledge in the mystery of Christ, which in other ages was not made known unto the sons of men, as it is now revealed unto his holy apostles and prophets by the Spirit;* and Luke 12:12 says, *"For the Holy Ghost shall teach you . . ".* Luke 24:45 tells us, *"Then opened he their understanding, that they might understand the scriptures."* And Matthew 13:11 tells us, *".. . .Because it is given unto you to know the mysteries of the kingdom of heaven, but to them it is not given".* The Apostle Paul, who was also given the ability to understand the mysteries of God, wrote in Ephesians 3:3,4,8,9, *"How that by revelation he made known unto me the mystery; (.....Whereby,*

when ye read, ye may understand my knowledge in the mystery of Christ) Which in other ages was not made known unto the sons of men, as it is now revealed unto his holy apostles and prophets by the Spirit..........Unto me, who am less than the least of all saints, is this grace given, that I should preach among the Gentiles the unsearchable riches of Christ; And to make all men see what is the fellowship of the mystery, which from the beginning of the world hath been hid in God, who created all things by Christ Jesus." We are taught by scripture not to believe everything we hear or read. 1 John 4:1-2 warns, *"BELOVED, believe not every spirit, but try the spirits whether they are of God: because many false prophets are gone out into the world. Hereby know ye the Spirit of God . . ."* Scripture teaches us to prove what we hear and read by comparing it to what God tells us, and to be careful when asked to trust only in the wisdom of men. 1 Corinthians 2:13 tells us: *"Which things also we speak, not in the words which man's wisdom teacheth, but which the Holy Ghost teacheth; comparing spiritual things with spiritual."*

When we understand that scripture is a mystery which God hides from those who desire to negate the word of God, and we understand that God delights in unveiling its mystery to His children, we see yet another miracle which God provides for us. We also learn to appreciate the power and majesty in God's all encompassing and perfect plan of salvation which He instituted just for us. Thus as we begin to understand sin by proxy we not only have to protect ourselves from the sins of our forefathers, but we also have to *protect our children* from the sins *we* commit. 1 Timothy 4:13 tells us, *"Till I come, give attendance to reading, to exhortation, to doctrine."* And in 1Timothy 4:16, *"Take heed unto thyself, and unto the doctrine; continue in them: for in doing this thou shalt both save thyself, and them that hear thee."*

> *"For by one offering he hath perfected forever them that are sanctified. And their sins and iniquities will I remember no more."*
>
> *Hebrews 10:14, 17*

Chapter Six

<u>HOLY COMMUNION</u>

God graciously, and out of His perfect love and understanding, offers to forgive our sins. The pre-requisites for that forgiveness is that we acknowledge our sins, feel remorse for them, desire not to commit those sins again, and that we willingly forgive others. What so many forget is that not only must we acknowledge those sins we have committed but also those sins of omission which God would have liked us to do yet we did not. This is why it is so important that we learn God's words, and strive to understand all that He wants to tell us. Scripture, which is God's direct instruction and comfort, teaches us every nuance of God's plan for mankind and every nuance of how Satan will work to prevent that plan from being completed. It teaches us to look *inward* so we can spurn even those seven deadly sins which are often so elusive. Many wonder why scripture seems to indicate that so few will become the Bride of Christ. Yet as God's words unfold and we begin to recognize the perfection of the person God wants us to become, we realize that we have much to learn. As we adjust our thoughts and actions to God's words, we change. We shed our old nature and become more loving, more giving, more understanding, and take on the Christ-like nature God longs for. But if we don't know all the little parts which make up the whole, we do not have the tools by which we can grow into that nature. Scripture teaches this but it requires the Holy Spirit to awaken our understanding and open the mysteries of scripture for us to fully comprehend.

God will forgive almost anything but only if our hearts are right...only if we come to Him in humbleness, acknowledging our sins and feeling great remorse for having committed them. Many believe that to forgive others, we have to forgive their actions and then *forget* them. Yet scripture does not tell us that we have to forget. In fact, God gave us the ability to remember so we can avoid hurtful or dangerous situations in the future.

God understands that we do not and cannot always live up to the very principles we espouse. We cannot be perfect in the practice of all the aspirations set before us no matter how hard we try. Therefore God looks at our striving rather than at what we do. He sees that we commiserate about our failures even when we repent our mistakes and strive to do better in the future. Yet it is our failures which keep us humble, remind us that we need God, and how blessed we are to have been brought into our faith. Our failures impel us to appreciate the unconditional love so evident in the sacrifice God made when He provided us with the forgiveness of sin. Scripture tells us that when we have sinned, have repented with remorse, desire not to repeat that same sin, and have forgiven those who have trespassed against us, we will have received Holy Communion worthily and that God remembers that sin no more. In other words, our sin is forgotten. Hebrews 8:12 tells us, *"For I will be merciful to their unrighteousness, and their sins and their iniquities will I remember no more."* Hebrews 10:14, 17 also tell us, *"For by one offering he hath perfected for ever them that are sanctified. And their sins and iniquities will I remember no more."* When our children act in ways which are not pleasing to us, we may reprimand them but when they ask for forgiveness and strive to make corrections, we forgive them and easily forget the indiscretion. But sometimes, situations arise which require us to remember what occurred in order to protect ourselves and others from future harm. In general, forgetting past indiscretions helps us find peace. But, as in all good things, sometimes we expand one good point into 'rules' which bring more harm than good. We misunderstand the proper context of the original thought and increase our anxieties by an unnecessary ideology which we find difficult to fulfill. The truth is that God gave us our memories for a reason. When we remember, for instance, how badly it hurt when we touched a hot stove, we are careful not to touch a hot stove again. We use our memories to keep us from those things which bring us harm. Our memories also enhance our faith and help us make the tough choices when we must act out of our faith. Faith is actually the *memory* of (trust in) what God has done for us. Hebrews 11: 7, 8 reminds us, *"By faith*

Noah, being warned of God of things not seen as yet, moved with fear, prepared an ark to the saving of his house; by the which he condemned the world, and became heir of the righteousness which is by faith. By faith Abraham, when he was called to go out into a place which he should after receive for an inheritance, obeyed and went out, not knowing whither he went." These verses tell us that faith provides the strength to act as God asks rather than as our inclinations might momentarily suggest. In fact when we have been harmed by someone and want to strike back, God tells us that *He* will take vengeance, but that we should not. What this provides for us an absence of guilt. God wants us to have peace and joy in our lives. To have peace, we cannot carry guilt, especially when that guilt is misplaced or the result of Satan's activities. Remembering the *danger* from such harm however is a protective measure and a healthy practice as long as we have forgiven the soul for committing that deed. The keywords here are, 'if we have forgiven them.' God wants us to forgive, but He has *not* asked us to forget. When God tells us to arm ourselves to fight the spiritual wickedness which seeks to devour us, the armour He speaks of is His words. His instruction is our protection. When our heart is right with God and we learn and do what He asks of us, His direction and protection is ours. He protects us from dangers, but warns us that we have a responsibility to be prudent, to be aware of evil, and to 'watch' for evil.... and flee it. We cannot watch for what is forgotten. 1 Peter 4:7 tells us, *"But the end of all things is at hand; be ye therefore sober, and watch unto prayer."* 1 Peter 5:8 says, *"Be sober, be vigilant, because your adversary the devil, as a roaring lion, walketh about, seeking who he may devour."* False prophets will come and we must watch for them so we do not fall prey to their teachings. Evil circles and tempts us and we must remember their end, so we are not tempted. Even family members may denounce God and scripture warns of this in Matthew 10:21:

"....children shall rise up against their parents and cause them to be put to death." Thus we must remember just as we must forgive. We must be watchful and careful just as we are forgiving and loving. We must not let our guard down as these end times are fulfilled, for God clearly warns in Mark 13:20: *"And except that the Lord hath shortened, those days, no flesh should be saved; but for the elect's sake, whom he hath chosen, he hath shortened them."* While here on earth, God offers us the forgiveness of our sins through the sacrament of Holy Communion. A sacrament, or covenant with God contains certain rules for receiving the gifts we are offered from such a bond. Holy Baptism, Holy Communion, and Holy Sealing are the three sacraments which re-institutes man access to God. They are prerequisites to being invited into the new kingdom which God is establishing for those who love Him. Scripture tells us why these sacraments are necessary and how they provide the means by which we can escape the captivity of

Satan and return to God. Scripture explains how the sin of Adam and Eve destined man to experience evil and denied them access to God. The sacraments allow us to obtain God's protection, avoid the traps laid by Satan, escape the consequences of our sins and the sins of our forefathers, and become pleasing in the sight of God.

The sacrament of **Holy Baptism** is given to break the captivity of inherited sin inflicted upon mankind by the sin of Adam and Eve which took away man's access to His Holy presence. **Holy Communion** offers us the forgiveness of sin through the sacrifice of Christ, requires a true acknowledgement and repentance of our sins, and provides the strength to avoid those sins in the future. **Holy Sealing** is the gift of the Holy Spirit which is bestowed on us to teach us, guide our steps and protect us from spiritual harm. These are precious gifts which must not be grieved by our lack of knowledge and lack of obedience to the word of God. Hosea 4:6 clearly warns: *"My people are destroyed for lack of knowledge; because thou hast rejected knowledge, I will also reject thee......"* 2 Corinthians 2:11 warns: *"Lest Satan should get an advantage of us: for we are not ignorant of his devices."* And Matthew 12:31 clearly warns: *"Wherefore I say unto you, All manner of sin and blasphemy shall be forgiven unto men; but the blasphemy against the Holy Ghost shall not be forgiven unto men."* Thus, those things which God tells us through scripture are provided to help us return to God and remain with Him for all eternity.

The path to God can be navigated by knowing God's words. Without this knowledge and the covenants or sacraments God offers, we cannot be free of sin nor understand godly love and cannot become the Bride of Christ.

> *"My people are destroyed for lack of knowledge; because thou hast rejected knowledge, I will also reject thee….."*
> *Hosea 4:6*

Chapter Seven

<u>WHAT IS GOD'S PLAN?</u>

As we read scripture, the beautiful plan which begins and ends with God's desire for the future of mankind is unveiled for us. God, knowing that man would sin, arranged for him to learn of good and evil so he would have the opportunity to freely choose good, repent of all evil, and seek the forgiveness of his sin and a life with God. Scripture teaches us that God longs to fill His kingdom with souls who will truly love one another, and love His Son and Him above all things. Matthew 22:37-39 says, "*Jesus said unto him, Thou shalt love the Lord thy God with all thy heart, and with all thy soul, and with all thy mind. This is the first and great commandment. And the second is like unto it, Thou shalt love thy neighbor as thyself.*"

God wants these souls to understand the value of love, trust, and loyalty, and to practice these attributes *voluntarily*. (John 14:23) God began His plan by creating the earth in its limited universe. Then He created Adam and Eve to live happily in the Garden of Eden, walking and talking with Him. But the angel Lucifer, later known as Satan, rebelled against God because he was jealous of Christ, and of the new being, man, who God planned to elevate above the angels. (Isaiah 14:12-15) As a result of his rebellion, Satan was thrown to earth with the angels who followed Satan and thereby also disobeyed God. (Revelation 12:9) These numbered one-third of all the angels.

Satan knew God's plan and understood that when the plan was completed, and God had obtained the number of faithful loving souls He longed for, Satan would be thrown into Hell for what he had done and with him all evil would be forever bound. To prevent God's plan from moving forward and thus forestall his own destruction, Satan destroyed God's relationship of trust and loyalty with Adam and Eve by enticing them to sin through disobedience. Satan knew that sin would automatically separate man from God because He knew that God labored under perfect righteousness. Thus, God was required to banish Adam and Eve as he had banished Satan. (Genesis 3:1 and Genesis 3:23) But God, knowing what Satan would do, had already provided a way for Adam and Eve, and the generations to follow, to escape the captivity of Satan through the sacrifice which Christ would bring for the forgiveness of sin which would break the captivity of Satan and allow man to return to God.

Christ offered Himself as the perfect sacrifice by which the sins of man could be forgiven. (John 1:29) At every turn, Satan interfered with God's plan, trying to destroy those who tried to follow God, because when God collected the number of souls He desired for His new creation, Satan would be bound forever. Thus Satan is fighting for his life when trying to draw us into sin.

However, because of God's love many of those tested by Satan are strengthened through his attacks, becoming like gold refined in the fires of tribulation. From these faithful, God is building what the Bible calls The Bride of Christ. In His quest that every man be afforded the same opportunity to return to God, God also provided for those who died in sin both before and after Christ brought His sacrifice. He did this by creating a means of testimony in eternity while grace is still available on earth. To fulfill this promise, Christ entered hell after His death to give testimony of His triumph to those who had died in their sins before He could bring His perfect sacrifice. (Luke 24:46) He told them that now they too could find forgiveness. (1Timothy 2:4) Then Christ went to His Apostles and commissioned them to teach God's children of His sacrifice for them and to also teach them to pray for those who died in sin.

A specific amount of time has been allotted in God's Plan of Salvation for His chosen ones to be made ready. (Acts 1:6-7) When that time is up, God will send His Son back to earth for the First Resurrection (Revelation 20:5) when He will take to heaven both those from eternity who have obtained forgiveness and those alive who have remained faithful. (11 Peter 3:10) When they are gone, grace will also be gone, and the final destruction of the end times will begin on the earth where, among other things, one-third of all the people on earth will die. When the destruction ends, God will send His Son back to earth with those He had taken at the

First Resurrection. They will have celestial (perfect) bodies, and will reign with Christ as kings and priests for one thousand years of peace where they will bring testimony to everyone living or dead who was not taken in the First Resurrection. Satan will be bound during this time, unable to influence mankind, so all mankind will learn about and accept God. But, after the one thousand years of peace, Satan will be loosed again for a little while so those who have now accepted God can also be tested. (Revelation 20:7) Satan will wreak havoc on those not firm in their faith and many will leave God to follow Satan. (Revelation 20:2)

Then the Day of Judgment will arrive when everyone, except those taken by Christ in the First Resurrection, will be judged. Those who accepted Christ and remained faithful after Satan was loosed again are termed the "lambs" in scripture and they will be allowed to occupy the new heaven God is creating. But others, who scripture calls the "goats", will be cast into hell with Satan forever. The goats, and Satan and his angels, will be cast into the lake of fire and brimstone and tormented day and night forever. (Revelation 20:10 and 15)

Those who were taken in the First Resurrection will continue to reign with Christ in the new kingdom. They will never have to be judged because their sins were forgiven, and entirely wiped away by God. Heaven rejoices in these who remained faithful to God from the beginning. These souls are the specific number of souls which scripture refers to who are called the Bride of Christ. These souls are also mentioned in the Apocrypha.

11 Esdras 2:40-41 says, *"Receive they number O Sion, and embrace those of thine that are clothed in white which have fulfilled the law of the Lord. The number of thy children whom thou longest for, is fulfilled: beseech the Lord that thy people, which have been called from the beginning, may be*

hallowed." Our desire is to work toward the completion of God's work here on earth, labor in faith, love, and charity to make ourselves worthy to be a child of God.

We strive to learn God's words, put on the armor of God, seek forgiveness, be an overcomer, and wait patiently for the completion of God's Plan of Salvation and the return of His Son.

We carry the hope in our hearts that soon God will find the last soul and we work to help find that last soul through our testimony. Romans 8:25 tells us, *"But if we hope for that we see not, then do we with patience wait for it."*

"He that overcometh shall inherit all things; and I will be his God, and he shall be my son."

Revelation 21:7

Chapter Eight

WHO WILL BE THE BRIDE?

Another of the precious gifts God has provided for us is the promise that if we strive to learn and do what He asks, He will reward us immensely. In Matthew 25:21 God says, *".....Well done, thou good and faithful servant: thou hast been faithful over a few things, I will make thee ruler over many things: enter thou into the joy of thy lord."* Scripture tells us that God refers to us as His children, and wants us to mature in faith so that we can develop into the bride of Christ. These descriptions present an expectation of an expanding maturity as we grow from child to bride. Scripture further supports this expectation in 1 Corinthians 13:11 saying: *"When I was a child, I spake as a child, I understood as a child, I thought as a child, but when I became a man, I put away childish things."* Scripture often uses the word "overcomer" in reference to God's children. Revelation 2:11 tells us *"....He that overcometh shall not be hurt in the second death."* Revelation 2:26 promises, *"And he that overcometh and keepeth my works unto the end, to him will I give power over the nations."* Revelation 3:5 tells us, *"He that overcometh, the same shall be clothed in white raiment; and I will not blot out his name out of the book of life, but I will confess his name before my Father, and before his angels."* Revelation 21:7 says, *"He that overcometh shall inherit all things; and I will be his God, and he shall be my son."* In Revelation 7:13 we read, *"......What are these which are arrayed in white robes? And whence came they?"* Revelation 7:14 answers saying, *"....These are they which came out of great tribulation, and have washed their robes, and made them white in the blood of the Lamb."* A white robe is the symbol of an unblemished soul which has had its sins forgiven. The blood of the Lamb is the sacrifice of Christ and the word "washing" is indicative of two processes which go hand in hand. The first requires the acknowledgement of one's sins, feeling remorse for them, striving to overcome the tendency to commit them again, and succeeding in much of that striving. The second part is the accepting and partaking of the sacrament of Holy Communion provided by the sacrifice of Christ and is the actual washing or cleansing of our sins. This takes place worthily through the actions mentioned in part one *and* our willingness to forgive those who have trespassed against us. Perfection cannot be attained while we are in the flesh and in Satan's territory. But God rewards our contrition and diligent striving and our thankfulness for the forgiveness of sin by one last act of Holy Communion before the Bride ascends. This knowledge helps us to develop into the overcomer who has made the necessary changes in their life whereby former ways and former temptations have been laid aside and we *work* toward godly behavior. Romans 12:2 tells us: *"Be not conformed to this world; but be ye transformed by the renewing of your mind, that ye may prove what is that good and acceptable and perfect will of God."* Galatians 5:1 warns, *"Be ye not entangled again with the yoke of bondage."* This indicates that it is possible to become entangled again even after we break away from sin and God himself frees us. Thus, to be an overcomer, we need to protect ourselves from the traps which might once again engage us. God provides us with information about how we can reach this goal. The armour of God is mentioned often throughout scripture and tells us that God, aware of our fragility, offers us protection. Ephesians 6:11 clearly says, *"Put on the whole armour of God, that ye may be able to stand against the wiles of the devil.* " This tells us that without this armour we may not be able to stand against evil. Further, Romans 13:12 teaches, *"The night is far spent, the day is at hand; let us therefore cast off the works of darkness and let us put on the armour of light.* " This warns us that there is not much time left before Christ returns. The armour itself is righteousness and cannot be obtained without the faith which comes from our relationship with God. That relationship is developed by learning of God, knowing what He asks of us, striving to do what He asks, communing with Him and having our sins forgiven. The word "darkness" is indicative of all things evil while the word "light" represents Christ and all He taught, and sacrificed for us. To obtain the armour of God, we must denounce all things which are the works of darkness and embrace all things which Christ brought us. When we have done our best to work toward this goal, God will empower us to withstand evil even when it is at its peak. 1 Corinthians 6:7 says, *"By the word of truth, by the power of God, by the armour of righteousness on the right hand and on the left."* If we have done due diligence and obtained the armour God offers, He promises that we will withstand the evil which will attack with a vengeance at the end of days. These end times will bring a great tribulation upon the entire world and occur just before Christ returns. It will be difficult for even the children of God to withstand. Ephesians 6:13 tells us, *"Wherefore take unto you the whole armour of God, that ye may be able to withstand in the evil day, and having done all, to stand."* Revelation 7:16-17 tells us: *"They shall hunger no more, neither thirst any more, neither shall the sun light on them, nor any heat. For the lamb which is in the midst of the throne shall feed them, and shall lead them unto living fountains of waters; and God shall wipe away all tears from their eyes."*

> *"But of that day and hour knoweth no man....but my Father only."*
>
> *Matthew 24:36*

Chapter Nine

WHAT IF I AM NOT TAKEN?

Most of us agree that the times in which we live are the end times of which the Bible speaks. Despite this awareness few rush to assess their spiritual condition. Nor do they assess the spiritual condition of those for whom they are responsible. Caught up in the harried pace of life and too busy to give God that which He asks, these believers may lose their soul salvation. Amazingly the Bible describes the conditions of the world when Christ returns and clearly predicts that many will be so engaged in their daily activities that they will be taken unaware and unprepared when the moment arrives. Matthew 25:40-42 tells us *"Then shall two be in the field; the one shall be taken, and the other left. Two women shall be grinding at the mill, the one shall be taken, and the other left. Watch therefore; for ye know not what hour your Lord doth come."* Sadly these verses and many others throughout scripture indicate that only half of those who believe they are ready for that day will be ready. Matthew 25:10-13 tells us: *"....they that were ready went in with him.....and the door was shut. Afterward came also the other virgins, saying, Lord, Lord, open to us. But he answered and said, Verily I say unto you, I know ye not. Watch therefore for you know neither the day nor the hour wherein the Son of man cometh."* There are many parables and instruction throughout scripture where we read that God has asked *all* men to make themselves ready by learning of Him and striving to do as He asks. Scripture clearly tell us that God wants all men to be saved. But as we read these parables and the words of the Apostles, we learn that though many are called, few will be chosen. We also learn that many will *not* accept God's invitation and will put forth a variety of reasons why they don't accept....some as simple as being "too busy"! Scripture also tell us that no one knows when Christ will return. We therefore must always be ready. Matthew 24:36 tells us, *"But of that day and hour knoweth no man...but my Father only."* We also read that when those who spurn God's invitation realize that they are not a part of the First Resurrection, they will be in great agony. Matthew 22:12-13 says, *"....how camest thou in hither not having a wedding garment?.....Bind him hand and foot, and take him away, and cast him into outer darkness; there shall be weeping and gnashing of teeth."* Scripture also tells us about the signs we will see as we approach the end times. Matthew 24:4-12,24 tells us, *"....wars, rumours of wars, famine, pestilences, earthquakes in diverse places, hatred toward Christians, betrayals hatred, false prophets with signs and wonders iniquity, no love"* Mark 13:12, 22 tells us, *"...brother shall betray the brother....father the son....children shall rise up against their parents....false Christ's and prophets...show signs and wonders".* Luke 21: 25 explains, *"And there shall be signs in the sun, and in the moon, and in the stars....the sea and the waves roaring....Men's hearts failing them for fear...."* And 2 Timothy 3:1-7 tells us, *"...in the last days perilous times shall come. For men shall be lovers of their own selves, covetous, boasters, proud, blasphemers, disobedient to parents, unthankful, unholy. Without natural affection, trucebreakers, false accusers, incontinent, fierce, despisers of those that are good. Traitors, heady, high minded, lovers of pleasures more than lovers of God; Having a form of godliness but denying the power thereof....ever learning, and never able to come to the knowledge of the truth."* 2 Esdras 16:24

from the Apocrypha adds: *"At that time shall friends fight one against another..."* We are also told about Christ's return to earth. 1 Thessalonians 4:16 tells us, *"For the Lord himself shall descend from heaven with a shout....then we....shall be caught up....to meet the Lord in the air....."* 1 Thessalonians 5:2 warns: *"For yourselves know perfectly that the day of the Lord so cometh as a thief in the night."* Scripture likens the invitation which God extends to all of mankind to a wedding where everyone in the town is invited to come yet most of the people invited were too busy, too tired, or too complacent to attend. Luke 14:16, 17, 24 explains, *"...a certain man made a great supper, and bade many......for all things are now ready........For I say unto you, That none of those men which were bidden shall taste of my supper."* Yet when the First Resurrection occurs, Christ will return to heaven with the faithful ....and all others will be left behind. 2 Peter 3:10, 14 tells us, *"But the day of the Lord will come as a thief in the night.....Wherefore, beloved, seeing that ye look for such things, be diligent that ye may be found of him in peace, without spot, and blameless."* The "wedding feast" will take place for three and one half years while the horrors of evil work upon the earth. After this time elapses, Christ and those He took at the First Resurrection will return to earth to bring testimony to all who had once spurned His teachings. Satan will be bound during this testimony and then loosed for a little while to test those who newly receive Christ's testimony. After this Satan will be bound forever. Revelation 20:1-2 tells us, *"And I saw an angel come down from heaven, having a key to the bottomless pit and a great chain in his hand. And he laid hold on the dragon, that old serpent, which is the Devil, and Satan, and bound him a thousand years. And cast him into the bottomless pit, and shut him up, and set a seal on him, that he should deceive the nations no more....."* Those who choose evil over good...even inadvertently.... will join Satan's final fate.

Revelation 21:6 tells us, *"And he said unto me, It is done.....He that overcometh shall inherit.....But the....unbelieving, and the abominable...and all liars, shall have their part in the lake which burneth with fire....."* Thus we know that great difficulties will come, but as we see them begin and our anxiety levels rise, it should act as a wake-up call. Acts 20:29 warns, *"For I know this, that after my departing shall grievous wolves enter in among you, not sparing the flock."* And Revelation 9:6 tells us, *"And in those days shall men seek death and shall not find it, and shall desire to die, and death shall flee from them."* Matthew 24:21, 22 warns, *"For then shall be great tribulation, such as was not since the beginning of the world to this time, no, nor ever shall be. And except those days should be shortened, there should no flesh be saved: but for the elect's sake those days shall be shortened."* While there may be very little time before we are caught up in the terrors predicted by scripture, we need to look carefully at our lives, take note of our shortcomings, and make the necessary corrections. Christ has taught us the principles which we must practice: love your enemies, do good to them that hate you, bless those who curse you, pray for those who despitefully use you, do to others as you would have them do to you, be merciful, judge not, condemn not, forgive, give, and rejoice in the Lord. (Luke 6). He has also taught us what sin is and how to obtain the forgiveness of sin. Scripture teaches us that sin covers many aspects and is not limited to things like murder and adultery but includes even our willful ignorance about God. We are to prepare our soul as meticulously as a Bride prepares for her wedding. If we fail to do this, if we are unprepared, have not developed as God has requested, when Christ arrives for the First Resurrection, we will be rejected. But for those who *are* prepared, God tells us not to fear those days. He encourages us throughout scripture to be courageous. Psalm 27:14 tells us, *"Wait on the Lord: be of good courage...."* Psalm 31:24 says, *"Be of good courage, and he shall strengthen your heart....*" Isaiah 12:2 tells us, "*Behold, God is my salvation; I will trust and not be afraid....*" 11 Chronicles 19:11 states, "*.....Deal courageously, and the Lord shall be with the good.*" There will be times when we are terribly frightened and times when our tears will flow and we will suffer. But, because of what we have learned we will know why, and will know that help is on its way. We can be comforted by God's words in Revelation 2:10: "*Fear none of those things which thou shalt suffer....*" And in Luke 12:32: "*Fear not, little flock; For it is your Father's good pleasure to give you the kingdom.*" And in John 14:27: "*......Let not your heart be troubled, neither let it be afraid.*" However, we have also been warned that if we are *not* prepared we cannot expect to be part of the First Resurrection. The parable of the five wise and five foolish virgins clearly demonstrates that for half of those who *proclaim* themselves a child of God, the door to salvation will *not* open to them. Matthew 25:1-13 tells this parable in its entirety and we read in Matthew 25:11, 12: *"......Lord, Lord, open up to us. But he answered and said, Verily I say unto you, 'I know you not."*

God is giving us a wake-up call and providing us with every opportunity to prepare for what is to come. Every one of us should be praying for the wisdom to understand what we need to do to be absolutely sure that we are prepared. In the end, we will experience the wonderful promise God reveals in Revelation 21: 4: *"And God shall wipe away all tears from their eyes; and there shall be no more death, neither sorrow, nor crying, neither shall there be any more pain....."*

Therefore, we should say as Joshua 24:15 says: *"...As for me and my house, we will serve the Lord"*. And while we wait we must... as John 16:33 and Acts 27:25 tell us: *"Be of good cheer"*.

> *"....walketh not in the counsel of the ungodly.... But delight in the law of the Lord."*
> *Psalms 1:1*

Chapter Ten

JUDGMENT DAY

There is a reason why God provides us with information about our future. He understands that as the end time prophesies are fulfilled the children of God will be persecuted and evil will prosper, thus He wants us to be assured that He will care for us during these times as well. By understanding God's plan of salvation and what He offers, and knowing that our suffering is for a limited time, we can withstand the days of evil and the wiles of Satan. God also wants us to understand death; the torment that death and the second death brings to sinners and the hope and joy offered to those who strive to be God's children. Those who remain faithful to Him and have their sins forgiven will receive rewards which are so great that they are beyond description. Throughout scripture God provides us with a glimpse of the new heaven and earth to strengthened us and show us the incredible wonder of what He wants to give us. For example, the Apostle John, while on the island of Patmos, wrote about streets paved in gold. This was an analogy to help us comprehend the immense beauty of the City of God which those who remain faithful will enjoy. God calls the people who will be given these gifts His firstfruits and while others may enter heaven, this group will live and reign at God's side as the Bride of Christ, the overcomers, the kings and priests of His new world. The information God provides for His children through scripture includes a description of what happens to them after death. Scripture explains that when Christ returns we will be given a celestial body which will never know sickness, sorrow, or death. 1 Corinthians 15:22 says, *"For as in Adam all die, even so in Christ shall all be made alive.* 1 Corinthians 15:35 says, *"But some man will say, How are the dead raised up? and with what body do they come? Behold, I shew you a mystery;* and 1 Corinthians 15:51 tells us, *"We shall not all sleep, but we shall all be changed."*

These verses tell us that all men must die to their dam-like nature, but that those who follow Christ will be made alive and will be changed. When we rise again after death we will be transformed from a terrestrial or natural body to a celestial or spiritual body. 1 Corinthians 15:40 tells us, *"There are also celestial bodies, and bodies terrestrial: but the glory of the celestial is one, and the glory of the terrestrial is another."* And 1 Corinthians 15:44

says, *"It is sown a natural body; it is raised a spiritual body. There is a natural body, and there is a spiritual body."* 1 Corinthians 15:47-49 tells us, *"The first man is of the earth, earthy; the second man is the Lord from heaven....And as we have borne the image of the earthy, we shall also bear the image of the heavenly."* This is an incredible promise and revelation, but there is also a warning which tells us that we must labor for this gift by being faithful, and by striving to learn of God and do as God asks. 1 Corinthians 15:58 tells us, *"Therefore, my beloved brethren, be ye steadfast, unmoveable, always abounding in the work of the Lord, forasmuch as ye know that your labour is not in vain of the Lord."* Psalm 1:1-3 tells us, *"Blessed is the man that walketh not in the counsel of the ungodly, nor standeth in the way of sinners, nor sitteth in the seat of the scornful. But his delight is in the law of the Lord; and in his law doth he meditate day and night. And he shall be like a tree planted by the rivers of water, that bringeth forth his fruit in his season; his leaf also shall not wither, and whatsoever he doeth shall prosper."* Here we learn who God will bless and thus what our behavior must be to be worthy of the celestial body which will rise at the First Resurrection. Although we all must die because of Adam, in Christ we will be made alive again. Psalms 1:1 tells us: *"walketh not in the counsel of the ungodly......but delight in the law of the Lord."*

The children of God await the return of Christ who will take from the earth those who are worthy to become His Bride. They understand that God wants a bride for His Son who is filled with the desire and ability to love. Thus, God's children strive to overcome the self-serving Adam-like nature and develop a Christ-like nature to achieve this goal. They understand that a loving father who seeks a bride for his son would want that bride to be kind, longsuffering, and forgiving. They also know that scripture warns that perhaps only half of those who are believers will meet the criteria required to become the Bride, causing us to wonder what will happen to those who, like the five foolish virgins, are left behind. These five foolish virgins were believers, but not prepared for the arrival of the bridegroom, thus not allowed to go with Christ when He came. (Matthew 1:1-13, and 24:40-41) The Bride will be those whom God deems the "firstfruits" or the "overcomers" and come from both the faithful still living on earth and the faithful from eternity. To be a part of the Bride of Christ is the hope of all the children of God and requires the development of the Christ-like gentle nature of perfect love and goodness, and the spurning of *all* things evil. This requires faith and love and the desire to be pleasing in the eyes of God. Although not all who believe will be found worthy to become the Bride of Christ, our Heavenly Father longs for all men to be saved. He has made provision that during the Thousand Years of Peace those not taken at the First Resurrection will have the opportunity to come to Christ and remain firm when Satan is loosed again. When Satan is loosed many will lose their faith, and hatred and unbelief will gain in power once again and overcome many souls. Satan will have such great power that these new believers will be sorely tested. And many will fall. When judgment day arrives, each will be judged based upon their faith and past deeds. *Every deed will be seen, weighed and judged* except for those who were taken at the First Resurrection whose sins were no more remembered. Once all judgment has been issued, those who have done their best to remain faithful will become what scripture calls a lamb and enter heaven. But if judgment day proves them unworthy, they will become what scripture calls a goat and experience the second death. The lambs will be allowed to enter heaven, but not the City of God where the family of God will reside. The goats who allowed sin and hatred to govern their lives will be sent to the Lake of Fire for the second death where they will be in torment for all eternity. Thus, though not all are called to be the Bride, many will be a part of the kingdom of God, but many will be cast into the Lake of Fire with Satan. The second death is separation from God and from love *for all eternity* because the soul never dies. There is *no* redemption from the second death, it is torment; it is life surrounded only with evil and it is for all eternity; it is forever. These words may seem harsh but are a reminder that not all believers will be a part of the First Resurrection and become a part of the Bride of Christ and thus the family of God. We need to clearly understand this so we strive harder to shed our old nature, become more like Christ, desire to leave all things evil and learn to love. Really love. Superficial love is not acceptable; it must be genuine and from the heart which God can read accurately. (1 Corinthians 13:13 and 1 Corinthians 13:1-3)

What then is real love? How can we test our level of love? Perhaps we believe that we love if we hold fellowships in our home…..but who do we invite? Only those who have a similar level of education, status, manner of dress, financial assets? Or do we also include the lonely, the poor, the heavily burdened, the jobless, the sick? Do we believe that we love because we help with church activities…..but have formed a clique and push some away? Do we believe that we love because we tithe…..and never help someone who lost their job or cannot provide a Christmas or Birthday gift for their children? Do we include the widow and widower, the never married, those divorced and those who struggle to speak our language? Scripture tells us that faith without works is dead. But what are those works? Are they works of love? Are they self sacrificing as Christ's love was for us? Or are our works judgmental or provided so that we gain personal accolades? Is our home open to everyone, and do we gladly bear one another's burdens and assist them through those burdens without judgment? Not all of us can do all things, but we must ask ourselves if what we *can* do is done with love and not to impress. God sees everything including the hidden recesses of our heart. He knows our motives and our faults and failings. However, God also knows our striving and hears our prayers to love more, and to grow in compassion, to learn what He asks of us. He knows that some people are difficult to love, but His heart is moved when we forgive and overlook. Our Heavenly Father also understands that some of us are action-oriented and some are behind-the-scenes people. He sees both efforts and rewards them equally. If we are older and all we can do is send little notes of encouragement, or make a phone call to an invalid, God is overjoyed. We do not have to do large things, as long as we demonstrate our willingness to do our *best* to love Him and those He loves. The Bride of Christ will be expected to be perfect in her love toward others by being, applying, developing, teaching, and giving love. When we truly love, we automatically desire to spurn what is not righteous in the eyes of God. We long to be with Him for all eternity where love will reign and evil will not exist. But if we spurn that which God offers and what is asked of us we may face the second death in the Lake of Fire which is a state of existence in a place without God, without righteousness, and devoid of love. It is the final and forever separation of good and evil. It is a place of torment, a place filled with anger, hate, jealousy, envy, intrigue, back-biting, slander, lies, plots, terror and all things evil. It is a place to be avoided with every ounce of our being.

But God wants us to be free of evil and to live with Him for all eternity in righteousness and love. He gives us every tool to do so. God's love for us is so great that He sent His Son to give His life so we could be saved from the captivity of the sin which dooms us to the Lake of Fire. He has given us the gift of scripture to help us learn. He wants all men to be saved and He wants us to succeed. He tells us in Jeremiah 31:3: *The Lord hath appeared of old unto me, saying Yea, I have loved thee with an everlasting love: therefore with lovingkindness have I drawn thee.* And He tells us in Revelation 22:17: *"And the Spirit, and the bride say, Come and let him that heareth say, Come, and let him that is athirst come. And whosoever will, let him take the water of life freely."*

It does not matter what sins we have committed in the past if we now decide that we want to learn of God and follow His precepts. God forgives us and He gladly teaches us. Under His love and guidance we can grow into the people He longs to have with Him forever.

Bibliography

The Holy Bible, King James Version, published by The New Apostolic Church, Canada, Thomas Nelson, Inc., Camden, NJ, 1972

James Strong, LLD, STD, *Strong's Exhaustive Concordance of the Bible*, Abington, Nashville, thirty fourth printing 1996, copyright 1890

Henry H. Halley, *Halley's Bible Handbook*, Zondervan Publishing House, Grand Rapids, Michigan, 24th edition, Copyright 1965

Henry M. Morris, *Many Infallible Proofs*, Moody Press, Chicago, 3rd printing 1977

Henry M. Morris, *The Bible and Modern Science*, Moody Press, Chicago, 1951, 1968

Donald Grey Barnhouse, *The Invisible War,* Zondervan Publishing House, Grand Rapids, Michigan, 12th printing 1976 copyright 1965

Robert Boyd, *Boyd's Bible Handbook*, Eugene, Oregon: Harvest House, 1983

Websters New Ninth Collegiate Dictionary, Mirriam-Webster, 1986

Roget's II The New Thesaurus, Houghton Mifflin Company, Boston, 1980, by the editors of *The American Heritage Dictionary.*

About The Author

Helen Gumienny Glowacki is an interior designer, writer, teacher, and motivational speaker. She was the host, writer, and producer of the television series "The Contemporary Woman", broadcast by UA Columbia Cablevision. Her writing credentials include an extensive background as a freelance feature and staff writer for four newspapers and for various newsletters and magazines. A graduate of William Paterson University, Helen received a Bachelor of Arts degree, magna cum laude, in Communications. She also received an Associate of Science degree with honors and is a registered nurse. She donates her books to cancer centers, drug rehabilitation centers, prisons, youth centers, hospitals, and also to the mission schools of *The Henwood Foundation* to use her gift for writing to help others find the love and comforting presence of God. She also emails books to those who are willing to receive testimony or will help in the quest to bring testimony to others. Helen writes amazing articles filed with insight about scripture and how God wants us to conduct our lives and posts many on Face Book and on her website. Those who have provided reviews of Helen's books tout the beauty of the stories in her novels and many have noted her non-fiction books "spiritually uplifting and biblically correct". Her greatest joys are her husband, two children, four grandchildren, and time spent in her New Apostolic faith and in fellowship.

To order additional books, to become a distributor of these books, or for more information: Visit the author's website at: www.helenglowacki.com or email the author at: helen@helenglowacki.com.

Excerpt from: "Caleb's Testimony"

Ann and Caleb believed that they trusted God implicitly, but when tragedy struck, and they were faced with losing everything they owned, they recognized the conditional nature of their faith. Stunned by their anger they were forced to reassess their commitment to God if He reclaimed every blessing He had bestowed upon them. Had their reaction provided Satan with a foothold on their heart? Was the blessing to be found in recognizing their spiritual shortcomings? Did God really want to remove those blessings? Were they being asked to overcome their newfound shortcomings? Did Abraham have similar thoughts when asked to give up his son? Did the rich man who was asked to leave his riches to follow Christ have these same thoughts? Could they willingly surrender what made their life comfortable? What would happen if they couldn't? As they labored through Caleb's long and painful recovery, they learned the importance of surrendering the pride of ownership if they wanted to become worthy. This eighth novel by Helen Glowacki is another heartwarming story with wonderful insight into how God works in our everyday lives and demonstrates what we may still need to learn, and how every tragedy can become a blessing. **ISBN 978-0-9847-2119-1.**

List and Description of Novels by Helen Glowacki (Book Size 6 x 9)

When God Broke Grandma's Heart: (208 pages) Rising from sorrow to become a beacon of faith Grandma struggles in an abusive marriage until God moves her from unequally yoked and broken to the healing of His love and forgiveness. Her granddaughter Sarah learns where to find answers to her problems and carries that legacy to those she loves. **Paperback: ISBN 978-0-9847-2110-8**

When God Took Grandma Home: (260 pages) About the heartache of drug addiction, of the enemy who destroys children through drugs, why God allows righteous anger, why we should pray for those in eternity and a description an incredible experience of faith for Matt and Sarah about why God allowed such heartache to occur. **Paperback: ISBN 978-0-49847-2111-5**

When Grandma Chased the Spirits: (208 Pages) The magnetism of idolatry, it's invisible power, and the heartache of bearing a child out of wedlock brings debilitating panic attacks to Mary and affects her husband Kevin. When Matt and Sarah tell them about their faith, God engineers a miracle to solve what that they thought impossible to resolve. **Paperback: ISBN 978-0-9847-2112-2**

The Granddaughter and the Monkey Swing: (284 pages) A wedding, a broken engagement, renovating and decorating a home through Divine Proportion, the truth about Halloween, and the gift of role models create a tender story of friendship. Helping through the planning and problems of a wedding culminates in the unveiling of a secret. **Paperback: ISBN 978-0- 9847-2113-9**

Grandma's Little Book of Poetry: The Story of God's Plan of Salvation: (277 pages) This beautiful whimsical story for all ages, begins when Sarah finds a manuscript in Grandma's desk and recognizes the story Grandma read to her and Josh and Caleb when they were children. Angels watch the inhabitants below them struggle to find God. **Paperback: ISBN 978-0-9847-2114-6**

Abiding Faith, Hidden Treasure: (262 pages) Serving in Iraq, Jim loses his faith to see a loving God allow so much heartache. Barbara invites him to dinner where Grandma shows him why creation and evolution co-exist and God's enemy creates the injustices Jim blames on God. Letters from the grave bring an incredible experience of faith. **Paperback: ISBN 978-0-9847-2115-3**

**And Then They Asked God**: (295 Pages) When Rebecca and Jayden arrive at their college campus they are overwhelmed by betrayal. Losing the values Rebecca once cherished fills her with guilt so monumental that she cannot forgive herself. Chaldeth the evil angel is defeated when God's grace frees Jayden and brings Rebecca's recovery. **Paperback: ISBN 978-0-9847-2116-7**

**Caleb's Testimony**: (262 pages) Caleb would have taken bets on his ability to trust God explicitly....until his accident.. Now, he and Ann must face the wrath of Satan aimed at causing them to blame God for their misfortune. **Paperback: ISBN 978-0-9847-2119-1.**

List of the "Why God Why" mini-series by Helen Glowacki (5 ½ x 8 ½)

**To What Purpose**?: (126 pages) This first book in the _Why God Why_ series answers questions about why we are here, what we need to learn, and what God plans for us. It is an excellent book for testimony and one you will share with others. **Paperback: ISBN 978-1-4507-7580-9**

Why God, Why?: (126 pages) This second book in the *Why God Why* Series describes why we experience heartache, its purpose, and how to face it. It answers questions about God's plan for us and what we need to do to be found worthy. **Paperback: ISBN 978-1-4507-7581-6**

Why Trust Scripture?: (126 pages) This third book in the *Why God, Why* Series addresses the challenges against scripture, who wrote the Bible, the importance of the sacraments, what role Satan plays, and how health and the Bible are related. **Paperback: ISBN 978-1-4507-7582-3**

What Should I Know about Life after Death and the Coming Tribulation?: (126 pages) What occurs following death, what will happen during the tribulation, and what the seven seals could mean to us are explained in this fourth book of the series. **Paperback: ISBN 978-1-4507-7583-0**

What Does God Want Me to do Right Now?: (126 pages) A concise explanation of what God asks of us, how we can live up to His expectations what is required to become a part of the

Bride of Christ, and what God plans for the future with or without us. **Paperback: ISBN 978-1 4507-9076-5**

Do My Little Sins Really Count? (126 pages) Most of us believe that the little sins don't really matter but scripture explains why they do and teaches is about the seven deadly sins, sin by proxy, and sin by commission and omission which can affect whether or not we take Holy Communion worthily. **Paperback: ISBN: 978-0-9847-2117-7**

List of Non-Fiction Books
By Helen Glowacki (Book Size 5 ½ x 8 ½)

Politically Incorrect: The Get Some Gumption Handbook For When Enough is Enough: (406 pages) Fifty timely and controversial issues are examined under the politically correct approach and compared to what scripture tells us is the approach that God wants His children to take. **Paperback: ISBN 978-1-4507-9074-1**

Overcoming Depression: How To Be Happy: (258 pages) We all face heartache, and all feel sad from time to time. But depression lingers and can result from many different causes.

It can rob us of hope and destroy our relationship with God. Thus our Heavenly Father tells us through scripture how we can tap into His blessing and His direction and brings joy out of tribulation. **Paperback: ISBN 978-1-4507-9077-2**

**What No One Tells You About Addictions**: (216 pages) Discussing the merits of tough love, the selfish co-dependency of the enabler, what scripture tells us about spiritual warfare and invasion, and generational sin, make this book a must read. **Paperback: ISBN 978-1- 4507--9075-8**

Book Reviews

Reverend (District Apostle Ret.) Richard C. Freund, President of The New Apostolic Church, USA, Sea Cliff, New York: Magnificent writer, a story which makes the reader become emotionally involved, a joy to read, strong Christian values. *"When God Broke Grandma's Heart"*, best seller quality.

Reverend (District Apostle Ret.) Richard C. Freund, President of The New Apostolic Church, USA. Helen's new novel, *"When God Took Grandma Home"* "Delights, brings comfort to those who grieve. Inspires, gives insight into the after-life, masterful portrayal.

Reverend Andrew Muliokela: New Apostolic Church in Alexandria, Virginia, formerly from Zambia Africa: *The Granddaughter and the Monkey Swing* and this series of books are awesome! A journey unlike another, I was reading a great novel, learning about confidence, love and support but also learning Bible verses at the same time! Helen Glowacki teaches through her books and I recommend them 100%. You'll enjoy the journey!

Reverend Frederick Rothe, (Ret. New Apostolic Church, New York) Palm Beach Gardens Congregation, Florida: Spent 48 years serving God and another 30 in the congregation. These books contain an accurate account of what God wants of us and why we suffer. The application of scripture and the people in the stories stand for the principles God wants in all of us.

Reverend Kevin Speranza, New Apostolic Church, Palm Beach Gardens, Florida: *And Then They Asked God* so happy I read this, weaves, documents biblical precepts, addresses political correctness, moral & political corruption, biased teaching, insidious growth of socialism renamed progressivism, self-importance, guilt and its debilitating power. WELL DONE! Identifies danger, artfully and Biblically addresses them.

Reverend Luke Jansen, Sr. V. P., Medical Connections, Boca Raton, Florida: "To Ms. Glowacki, author of **The Grandma Series**: grateful for your books, refreshing to find a Christian author who sees the *difference* between religion and spirituality AND that the two can and should be used in the same sentence.

Reverend Derryck Beukes, Montana-De Aar Congregation, Northern Cape, South Africa: Dear Helen, I personally often use your articles in my soul care visits, especially where youth are involved. I can assure you that your articles made a difference to my way of thinking, and I am busy encouraging fellow priests to read your works, as they are so factual and insightful! Thank you for your hard work. I thank God for you, and the wisdom He gave you! Please continue with the excellent work.

Deacon Shadreck Wilima, Overspill Congregation, Ndola, Zambia: Your articles prompt realistic examples which New Apostolic Christians need for their everyday living.

Youth Chairperson, Sunday School Teacher, Mulenga Ernest, Lusaka Central Congregation, Lusaka, Zambia: Through your writing I am constantly reminded of what to be aware of. I pray that God keeps you in the hollow of His hand, guards you and guides you to reach your brethren as you do me. Thanks for caring for the souls of many.

Reverend Aurelio Cerullo, Atripalda Congregation in Campania, Southern Italy: Dear Helen, your books and articles, and social networking bring brothers and sisters the words of our faith and touch the hearts of those who do not know our faith. Our goal is found through the grace of the apostolate and in this sense, the word's from 1 Corinthians 15:58 assumes an important meaning: *"Therefore, my beloved brethren, be steadfast, immovable, always abounding in the work of the Lord, Knowing That your labor is not in vain in the Lord"*. Now that I am a minister of God for about a year I too am grateful to our beloved Father in Heaven for having opened the eyes of my soul, for having removed the plugs from my ears of my heart to hear and listen to His will in connection and communion with those who precede us, guided by the light of the Holy Spirit. God's work always evolves and adapts to the times and even via computers, cell phones and smart phones. I Thank God for having been able to know you, you're a very valuable pearl. God bless you richly.

Rev. Fred Krueger, (Ret.) Lutheran Minister 12 yrs and Clinical Social Worker 26 years, Dallas, Texas: "Inspiring, grabs the heart, author headed to the bestseller list, a pleasure to read, masterful. *"When God Took Grandma Home"* filled with insight into God's plan!

NOTE: The articles which are referred to in these reviews are excerpts from Helen Glowacki's non-fiction books. Not shown are reviews by the ministers who oversee *The Henwood Foundation*'s New Apostolic Mission Schools in Zambia and review all reading materials prior to distribution.

Edith Stier, wife of a Ret. District Evangelist, Clifton, New Jersey: *The Grandma Series* helps those in need, inspirational, heartwarming, ends with a beautiful example of how God explains our pain, renews hope, shows us the way, creates miracles. I love this series.

Patricia Robinson, wife of a Ret. Rector, Indiana: 5 star rating: *When God Broke Grandma's Heart*: WONDERFUL INSPIRATIONAL NOVEL, enjoyed this book, well written, Bible references, how to achieve peace of mind and soul.

Rosemarie Schaal, wife of an Ret. Reverend, New York: *Abiding Faith, Hidden Treasure:* Reader develops empathy, feels emotion, hears a battle between scientific and spiritual knowledge. Skillful, detailed, brilliant, vivid, teaches that nothing happens that is not planned by Him.

Colette van Loggerenberg, wife of a Minister, Scottsville Congregation of Pietermaritzberg, South Africa: *Grandma's Little Book of Poetry: The Story of God's Plan of Salvation:* This has to be one of the BEST EVER books that I have read....If you ever get the chance to get one of Helen's novels...READ IT. It's like a fairytale but a TRUE fairytale.....Close your eyes and picture this: Grandma with her hair in a bun, glasses perched delicately on her nose, sitting in a rocking chair and her grandchildren sitting on the floor with BIG eyes hanging onto her every word.....but with a twist!!!!! If you have doubts about PRAYER...read this book. I LOVED IT...thank you!

Debbie Espeland, wife of a Rector, Palm Beach Gardens Congregation, Florida: 5 star rating: *When God Took Grandma Home:* HEARTWARMING! This book touched my heart. It is both heartwarming and very spiritual.

Aletta Venter, wife of a Deacon, Scottsville Congregation, Pietermaritzburg, South Africa: *"Grandma's Little Book of Poetry: The Story of God's Plan of Salvation".* What a learning process for me. Oooh I just **love** the way the angels are telling the story, **very original!** When is mankind ever going to learn? The inhabitant's lesson was to learn of good and evil. And they failed miserably each time. The devil has his agenda, and the inhabitants are the target. They call upon God for help, the angels rejoiced. Great....!!!

Aletta Venter, wife of a Deacon, Pietermaritzburg, South Africa: *"Abiding Faith, Hidden Treasure"* is the deepest and most rewarding novel I have ever read, touched my soul, made me cry, author's understanding of God's work is astounding, opens the mysteries

Lisa Mayo, wife of Minister, Palm Beach Gardens Congregation, Florida: Helen's *Why God Why* series of books gave me a new understanding of my faith. They are informative, so enlightening and in-depth, but in a way that is easily understood!!

Tammera Shelton, M.S. Psychology, Odenton, Maryland: I find *"When God Broke Grandma's Heart"* inspirational, beautifully portrays need to let go of negative events and that despite injustice, no pain is for naught.

Robert W. Rothe, USMC 1970-1976, Nevada: 5 star rating: *When God Broke Grandma's Heart:* Outstanding writer, kept me riveted, an angel sent to help through trying days. Thank you for helping me find peace.

Katharina Leipp, Schopfheim, Germany: This is the first time I have ever heard of a female New Apostolic author and I am very impressed by your articles. I have sent your link to my Shepherd and German friends and would like you to consider advertising in our German *Our Family Magazine.*

Claudine Visagie, South Africa: I'm trying to think of a way to introduce Helen's books and articles to others… especially to our youth. They are life changing!

Rabecca Mukuta Mukato, Lusaka, Zambia, Africa: Speaking on behalf of my Dad, District Elder Mukato, your articles are brilliant because they have changed me! Because of your articles my Dad has less headaches!

Robert Henry Parkes, Pietermaritzburg, South Africa: You are gifted with the verses and writings you do and are so inspiring to others. God is really using you as His special servant. You are really a wonderful person and we thank the Lord for you our sister in faith.

Frank Geores, from Port St. Lucie, Florida: *"When Grandma Chased The Spirits:* beautiful spiritual experience, can see caring nature and loving heart of author, eloquently reveals her love for God and search for truth. Worthy of the Star of Bethlehem rating. Thank you for sharing your magnificent gift.

Ben Lodwick, Avid Reader., from Brookfield, Wisconsin: Wow! An eye opener about God's plan of salvation, and why bad things happen to good people. Reminds me of Jim LaHaye and Jerry B. Jenkins "Left Behind Series". MUST READ!"

Dr. Walter Forman From North Palm Beach, Florida: *Grandma's Little Book of Poetry: The Story of God's Plan of Salvation:* a "wonderful book about success and failure in life. All Helen's novels are wonderful, a balm for the soul and an education to the seeker."

Susan Day, From Jupiter, Florida: *Abiding Faith, Hidden Treasure* : I hated to put it down, couldn't wait to pick it up, read all Helen's books, proves every point, shows what to do through God's words. I am 90 and Helen's books have helped me call on God.

Georgette Rothe, From Fort Piece, Florida: *Abiding Faith, Hidden Treasure* was more than I expected; a Biblical course making you re-evaluate your beliefs, enjoyed the journey very much.

Fred D'Alauro, from Palm Beach Shores, Florida: Internet 5 star rating: *When God Took_Grandma Home:* Remarkable! Inspirational, moving. Fascinating storyteller with a real message.

Debra Forman, Chester, New York. Internet 5 star rating: *When God Broke Grandma's Heart:* Written from the heart, shares the strong beliefs that shelters us in times of need, courage captivates the reader. Thank you.

Anonymous: Internet 5 star rating: *When God Broke Grandma's Heart:* WHEN LIFE GETS YOU DOWN, PICK THIS BOOK UP, it wrapped its arms around me. A wonderful read. Congratulations on an inspiring work.

A reviewer, a reader in Kentucky: Internet 5 star rating: *When God Broke Grandma's Heart:* Well written, heartwarming, overcoming heartbreak through God, touches your heart. A worthwhile read for all generations.
A reader: Internet 5 star rating: *When God Broke Grandma's Heart:* a must read for all generations. FANTASTIC!

A reviewer Internet 5 star rating: *When God Took Grandma Home:* Moves you, captivating.

A reviewer, a Kentucky reader: Internet 5 star rating: *When God Took Grandma Home:* MUST READ! Touching story of life's tragedies and how lessons learned from these heartbreaking events can turn into blessings.

Characters in Helen Glowacki's Novels

Grandma: Grandma's life was filled with sibling betrayal and marital abuse. Her love of God, home remedies and famous boxing stance touches the heart.

Sarah: Sarah helps Grandma write her journal, learns about God's plan of salvation and the enemy who wants to harm her. She carries on Grandma's legacy of faith.

Matt: Matt, Sarah's husband, has a rock-like faith but when he loses a loved one, struggles with his anger with God, until he has a miraculous experience of faith.

Paul: Paul is Matt's older brother who earned a Captain's license for a seagoing tugboat. His faith sustains him despite enduring terrible circumstances.

Mary and Kevin: Mary and Kevin become Matt and Sarah's neighbors and friends. Mary's panic attacks end when God brings a miracle they never thought possible.

Elizabeth: Elizabeth adopts Rebecca, loses her husband twelve years later, is confronted with a potentially deadly illness and searches for Rebecca's birth mother.

Rebecca: Rebecca is Elizabeth daughter and Jayden's friend. Her father's death, the illness her mother faces, and a series of challenges at college almost destroy her.

John: John, a deacon, lost his wife to a debilitating disease, becomes Elizabeth's friend, and helps his daughter and grandson through a difficult divorce.

Jayden: Jayden is John's grandson and becomes Rebecca's friend. He has learned that prayer helps solve problems and he and Rebecca begin to share their faith.

Wade and Ruth: Wade is Jim's boss and friend who adopts two children from Iraq. Ruth is Jayden's mother and John's daughter who struggles to let go of the past.

Joshua and Debbie: Joshua, Sarah's younger brother, was demanding and judgmental until Caleb stepped in. Debbie looks to Joshua's family to be her role models.

Caleb and Ann: Caleb is Sarah and Josh's older brother and the family looks to him as they once looked to Grandma. Ann, Caleb's wife harbors a secret sadness.

Barbara and Jim: Barbara, Matt's sister is also Sarah's close friend. Her husband Jim plays devil's advocate in family debates, and matchmaker for his friend Wade.

Heza and Bara: Heza and Bara endured a suicide bomber attack when Bara was one and one half years old and Heza as she was born. They are adopted by Wade.

Chaldeth: Chaldeth is a fallen angel sent to destroy Grandma's family. He plots to bring great heartache to Rebecca and Jayden and their family to break their faith.

Durk: Durk, abused by a cruel father, is a sophomore at the college Rebecca and Jayden attend. He brings harm to Rebecca and Jayden but Jim gives him a second chance.

Professsor T. Nagorra, and Emils, and Dean Peerca: These tenured professors befriend Durk and engage in activities which harm the students and the college campus.

Professors Doog and Sendnik, and President Legna: These three share a faith in God, a love for their country, and desire to be role models. They help save the campus.

Richard and Rachel: Richard is a physician for whom Caleb built a house on the property next door to where he and Ann. live. Both couples share godly values and thus became friends.

Joe and Preacher: Both men work for the company which hired Caleb to supervise the construction of a shopping mall. Preacher is always trying to teach Joe what scripture says.